CREATIVE EDUCATION

EARLY SPORTS BOOKS

MEET THE CENTERS

by Linda Thomas

photographs from the National Hockey League

creative education
childrens press

Published by Creative Educational Society, Inc., 123 South Broad Street, Mankato, Minnesota 56001 Copyright © 1976 by Creative Educational Society, Inc. International copyrights reserved in all countries. No part of this book may be reproduced in any form without written permission from the publisher. Printed in the United States.

Library of Congress Cataloging in Publication Data
Thomas, Linda   Meet the centers.
SUMMARY: Biographical sketches of four hockey centers: Phil Esposito, Stan Gvath, Bobby Clarke, and Gil Perreault.
1. Hockey—Biography—Juvenile literature.
[1. Hockey—Biography]   I. National Hockey League.   II. Title.
GV848.5.A1M63   796.9'62'0922 [B]   [920]   76-20743
ISBN 0-87191-534-0

Phil Esposito gets more fan mail than any other professional hockey player. He is the most popular center in the NHL.

Phil has led the National Hockey League in scoring for five of the last seven years. He was the first center to make the all-star team six years in a row. He has also been named the Most Valuable Player twice.

Still, his slow skating fools many defensemen. Just when they think they can move in to take the puck away, he scores. Suddenly he has great strength, a keen eye and lightning reflexes.

The first professional hockey team that Phil played for was the Chicago Black Hawks. He was not a star with the Black Hawks. They traded him in 1967 to the team that finished in last place, the Boston Bruins.

In his first season with the Bruins Phil made 35 goals and 49 assists. For the first time in nine years the Bruins were in the play-offs.

The 1968-69 season was a year of records. Phil Esposito led the entire NHL with an unbelievable 126 points. He won the Ross Trophy for scoring and the Hart Trophy for Most Valuable Player.

The Bruins won the Stanley Cup during the 1969-70 season. It was the first time in 29 years!

Phil set three new records in the 1970-71 season. He scored the most goals and made the most points in a single season. Phil and his linemen made more goals than any other line in hockey history! The Bruins lost only 14 games all season.

Phil continued to play for the Bruins until the end of the 1976 season, when he was traded to the New York Rangers. Phil Esposito will always be one of hockey's greatest superstars.

STAN MIKITA

Stan Mikita is one of the most unusual and interesting players in hockey.

One interesting fact about Stan is the helmet he wears. He received an ear injury when a puck hit him in the side of the head during the 1967 season. In order to play the rest of the season he had to wear a helmet.

Stan decided he would wear a helmet, for his own protection, after this experience. He designed one that was both comfortable and practical. Now he wears his helmet during every game. A lot of the younger players also have started wearing helmets.

Stan designed the curved-blade stick. It lets him shoot off either foot while he is skating. It also helps him to control the puck better.

Stan and his teammate Bobby Hull were the first players to use the curved sticks. Now they are popular with many players.

Stan plays hockey with a combination of speed and aggressiveness. This style is very different from the way he played during his first years with the Chicago Black Hawks.

As a rookie, Stan played rough. He had 119 minutes in penalties that year. During the next few years his penalty minutes increased!

Stan finished the 1961-62 season with 77 points. He also made the all-star team.

Stan won the Ross Trophy for the third time in the 1966-67 season. The Ross Trophy is for the leading scorer in the NHL. He also won the Hart Trophy for Most Valuable Player and the Lady Byng Trophy for sportsmanship.

The next season Stan again won all three trophies. He was the first player in NHL history to win all three trophies two years in a row.

Bobby Clarke was listed as one of the five best amateurs in Canada. But he was not drafted until the second round when the Philadelphia Flyers selected him. Everyone was afraid that he would not be able to play because he had diabetes.

Bobby Clarke did not have a fantastic season as a rookie. He ended it with only 15 goals and 31 assists. The Philadelphia Flyers didn't even make the play-offs.

The 1971-72 season was a good one for Bobby. He made 35 goals and 46 assists. He won the Bill Masterton Trophy for courage. The season had been disappointing for the Flyers. They didn't make the play-offs. But Bobby was extremely popular with Flyer's fans. They liked his modest, friendly manner.

The Flyers were second in the 1972-73 season. Bobby won the Hart Trophy as Most Valuable Player in the NHL. It was the first time a player from the West Division received this trophy. He was also second in scoring.

Bobby was selected Captain of the Philadelphia Flyers in the 1973-74 season. That year the Flyers lost only 16 games and had 12 ties. It was the fifth-best NHL season record in NHL history.

The Flyers made the play-offs. When the final game was over Bobby Clarke and teammate Bernie Parent skated around the arena holding the Stanley Cup!

The Philadelphia Flyers were first in their division in the 1974-75 season. Once again they won the Stanley Cup. A hockey writers' poll selected Bobby Clarke as the hardest-working player in the NHL, the best penalty-killer, the best "defensive" forward, the best team leader and the best man on face-offs.

Bobby finished the 1975-76 season with 30 goals and 89 assists. The Flyers again made it to the Stanley Cup finals. But the Montreal Canadiens claimed the Stanley Cup. Bobby Clarke and the Philadelphia Flyers have set some fantastic records for the NHL, and they will be hard to top.

Gil Perreault is speedy and shifty. He can almost fake an opponent off his blades.

Gil has been playing for the Buffalo Sabres since 1970. He gave a fantastic performance as a rookie. He made 38 goals and 34 assists. This was a record for both goals and total points made by a rookie. He was also selected as Rookie of the Year and won the Calder Trophy.

After Rene Robert and Rick Martin joined the Sabres,
Gil really set records! People started calling Gil, Rene,
and Rick the "French connection" line. Gil won the
Lady Byng Sportsmanship Trophy in the 1972-73
season. He had a scoring total of 88 points and only
10 penalty minutes.

The French connection made 131 goals in the
1974-75 season. Gil Perreault was listed as the best
one-on-one forward in the NHL. He had made 39
goals.

The Buffalo Sabres finished the 1974-75 season at the top of their division. They were also second in the NHL. They lost the Stanley Cup to Philadelphia.

When the 1975-76 season arrived the Buffalo Sabres were listed as the biggest, fastest and newest team in the NHL. Even though they didn't have a very good season, Gil Perreault gave a great show as he carried the puck up the ice and made a lot of flashy detours. He is definitely one of the most spectacular one-on-one forwards in the NHL.

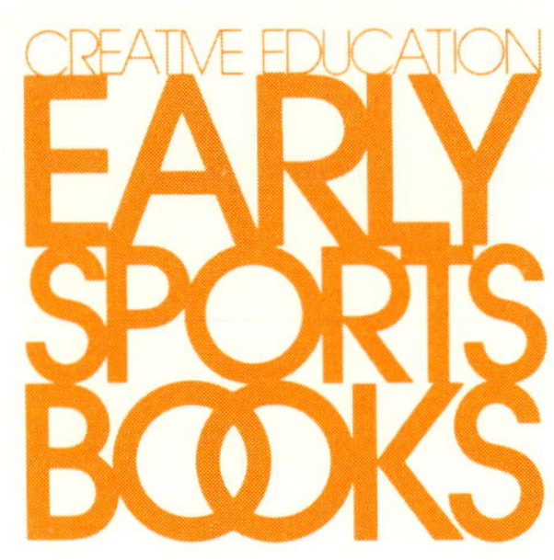

MEET THE COACHES
MEET THE LINEBACKERS
MEET THE RECEIVERS
MEET THE QUARTERBACKS
MEET THE RUNNING BACKS
MEET THE DEFENSIVE LINEMEN

MEET THE WINGMEN
MEET THE CENTERS
MEET THE DEFENSEMEN
MEET THE GOALIES

MEET THE INFIELDERS
MEET THE CATCHERS
MEET THE MANAGERS
MEET THE HITTERS
MEET THE PITCHERS